Writers of Wales

EDITORS

MEIC STEPHENS   R. BRINLEY JONES

THOMAS GWYNN JONES

1871–1949

Photograph by courtesy of Mr Emrys W. Jones

W. Beynon Davies

THOMAS GWYNN JONES

*University of Wales Press
on behalf of the Welsh Arts Council*

1970

77-850443

When the Reverend Rowland Williams, the Archdruid with the bardic name of Hwfa Môn, called out the pseudonym—Tír na n-Óg—of the successful author in the *awdl* competition for the chair in the Bangor National Eisteddfod of 1902, the poet himself was not there to answer the call, and only a very few people knew who he was. Professor John Morris Jones in his adjudication had given him high praise for his poem on the set subject, YMADAWIAD ARTHUR *(The Passing of Arthur)*, and had shown how different and better his poem was from the work of the other ten or so in the competition. "This poet", he said, "has been content to tell the romantic tale in the spirit and style of the world of the romances." And as the author of the poem, Mr T. Gwynn Jones, a young journalist from Caernarfon, was not present, a friend of his and a fellow journalist, Mr Beriah G. Evans, was chaired in his stead. It chanced that the author, though he had learnt secretly that his poem was adjudged the winning one, had gone off by train that morning to attend a wedding at Denbigh.

When the poem was eventually published in the EISTEDDFOD TRANSACTIONS volume it was seen at once to be exceptional in many ways. Hitherto for many years the successful poems for the chair and crown in the National Eisteddfod had been the work of poet-preachers, that is, clerics or ministers of the various denominations, and this held good for many years afterwards. But T. Gwynn Jones was a journalist with a different outlook, training and experience. The set subject for that year was also different from the type of subject set in previous years; there had been a strong tendency to set abstract or religious or Biblical themes like BEYOND THE VEIL, and the poems submitted were more often than not vague and long-winded meditations with little respect for form or for a precise use of language. And whereas these other efforts in their prosaic and essay-like treatments generally ran into lengths of between seven and eight hundred lines, YMADAWIAD ARTHUR by T. Gwynn Jones was a mere brief and sparing three-hundred-and-fifty. In short the poem was something new in the language, and as every student of modern Welsh literature knows, it marks the beginning of a new era in our poetry in subject, language and form.

In making the point that this ode by T. Gwynn Jones in the Bangor eisteddfod of 1902 marked a complete break with the 'traditional' eisteddfod poetry of most of the nineteenth century and began a new and vigorous movement in the Welsh poetry of this century, it must be explained that it had not sprung from nowhere. It was preeminently the product of a movement which had its origin in a return to the study of 'classic' Welsh prose and verse that had followed the forming of departments for the study of Welsh in the new colleges of the University of Wales. The pioneering work had been done mainly by Sir John Rhŷs at Oxford, and even in some continental universities, in the seventies and eighties. John Morris Jones, a pupil of Rhŷs and Professor of Welsh at Bangor, was a powerful influence in insisting that Welsh writers must return to a study of the 'classic' authors not only for their content as a source of inspiration but also for their style and metrical and syntactical patterns, such patterns being very much closer to those of the spoken language of the poet's time than a style imitative of English patterns which had become so prevalent in the course of the last century. And though T. Gwynn Jones was not a product of the University, he was by instinct a man of academic leanings, and he had fallen under the spell of this renaissance movement.

But whose was this voice raised in revolt against the accepted modes of the times? Thomas Gwynn Jones was born at Gwyndy Uchaf farm near Betws-yn-Rhos, Abergele in 1871, and as the family moved to other farms, he was educated at schools in Llanelian, Old Colwyn, Denbigh and perhaps Abergele. He probably worked at home on the land for a time, but he must have studied on his own and read very extensively. In 1890, when he was nineteen, he was taken on as a sub-editor by Thomas Gee in the office of Y FANER in Denbigh. Then in 1894 he moved to Liverpool to work on Y CYMRO under its editor, Isaac Foulkes, writing occasionally for Y FANER, THE LIVERPOOL MERCURY, THE LIVERPOOL POST, and the MANCHESTER GUARDIAN. After three years in Liverpool he returned to Denbigh to work on Y FANER.

Within the year he had moved, in 1898, to Caernarfon as sub-editor in the offices of YR HERALD GYMRAEG. Later, in 1907, he went to Y Wyddgrug (Mold) as editor of another weekly called Y CYMRO, returning to Caernarfon in the following year as editor of a local weekly called PAPUR PAWB. But he did not stay long with this paper for in the following year, 1909, he was given a post as cataloguer in the newly formed National Library of Wales in Aberystwyth.

As he had ended his formal education at the age of fourteen, the details given above are significant inasmuch as they show what work the poet did in this important period in his life, that between the age of nineteen and thirty-nine. Throughout this period he was a busy journalist or newspaper man, working in four different areas. He had not spent these formative years in a sheltered calling as a hermit, but had been busy collecting, arranging and composing reports on law court proceedings and political meetings, reports of strikes and important religious conventions, of funerals and weddings, of the war in South Africa and of discoveries of gold in the far corners of the world. He was a thoroughly experienced newspaperman who knew well how to produce a newspaper or a book, and in the course of these activities, he had met and come to understand a very great number of ordinary folk and of public figures.

So at the time of being declared the author of the best *awdl* in the Bangor eisteddfod of 1902 T. Gwynn Jones was an experienced journalist of thirty-one. He had already published a small volume of poetry when he was twenty-one, and it was evident from this that here was someone who had a great feeling for words and a cultivated and extensive vocabulary. Then in 1896–97 he had some substantial work published in the monthly CYMRU under the title GWLAD Y GÂN *(Country of Song)*, and this work, and other poems, were published under that title in 1902. Chief among them is the satirical poem entitled *Gwlad y Gân*. This work is about four-hundred-and-fifty lines, in verses of ten lines each, and is in three parts. In the first part, he pokes gentle fun at the eisteddfod establishment of the day, the petty foibles of the members of the Gorsedd, particularly the allegedly shady methods used by aspiring bards to succeed in poetry competitions. (The poet returned to this theme later in a hilariously funny novel he wrote about 1922.) In the second section of the poem he satirises the methods of newspapermen, particularly the pompous style of local and political correspondents. Lastly, he attacks the despicable Dic-Sion-Dafyddion, i.e., those Welshmen who, on prospering in the world, soon pretended to forget their Welsh, using only English, but who vaunted their love of the language on eisteddfod platforms or at St David's day Dinners: these he castigates without mercy. And as did his eisteddfod *awdl* this *Gwlad y Gân* poem showed a mastery of metre and language, particularly in the clever rhymes which are so effective in turning ostensibly 'serious' poetry into satire.

What in the poem YMADAWIAD ARTHUR had given the adjudicator cause for such praise? The theme was familiar, and had been the subject of one of Tennyson's well known poems. It would be tedious to repeat the story here, but I shall attempt to show briefly where Gwynn Jones's differs from other treatments of the theme.

In Tennyson's poem the action takes place on a frosty moon-lit night; Arthur, very much the king, addresses Bedivere in long formal speeches in the epic tradition (and sometimes makes one think of a Victorian nobleman giving instructions to his butler). In the ceremony on the barge, those on it are clad in black like a Victorian family funeral, all giving the impression of disconsolate gloom. In the YMADAWIAD ARTHUR of Gwynn Jones, on the other hand, the event happens on a bright and sunny day except for an occasional swift-moving cloud casting a fleeting shadow on the landscape. Bedwyr and Arthur are two intimate friends who had been in the same campaign, and their dialogue is brief, but fluent; then at the critical moment Bedwyr expresses his wish to accompany Arthur on the barge but is told by one of the maidens that he cannot do so; he must stay behind, for Arthur is never going to die. And in his farewell message to him, Arthur charges Bedwyr to be brave and cheerful though he will have to face much suffering. Briefly it runs:

"I am now going to Afallon to recover from my wounds. But I shall return and lead my country to victory when the time is ripe. Though this land will fall on evil days, poets from among the great nations of the world will sing its praises. It will suffer defeats and oppression, but in the end it will recover and renew its strength. On that day, a bell will ring, I shall grasp my sword once more and return to restore my people and language to their pristine glory."

Then the barge slid away leaving a bewildered Bedwyr on the shore. As the sail was hoisted, Bedwyr could hear very sweet singing being wafted towards him from the barge over the lake. It was the song of the three maidens in attendance on the King, and it tells of the beauty and charm and life-giving qualities of this isle of Afallon where Arthur was being taken. A verse translation by Mr D. Myrddin Lloyd conveys the meaning of this song: it does not, of course, try to reproduce the metrical intricacies of the original. The three verses run as follows:

AVALLON

Far over the wave lies a land of delight
Where grief lingers not, nor time's grey blight:
Men know no pain on that peerless shore,
Caressed by the breezes that play evermore:
Every heart is gay, and life is a song
In Avallon's isle all the day long.

A blissful land filled with dreams of old
That calmed our fears through ages untold;
Hopes and desires are treasured there,
And the fruits of our travail grow rich and rare;
There shame does not sear, and faith is strong,
And no hearts made weak by an ancient wrong.

On that island's shore burns the pure flame
Of the muse that oft to our poets came
With words of fire that men might arise
From the dust to a nobler enterprise.
Unwearied by age, or by grief and care,
The breath of the nation's life is there.

As the music ceased a fine mist spread over the lake, and soon the barge had disappeared in it. Bedwyr thereupon, full of unspeakable sorrow, returned to the scene of the battle.

As can be seen from this summary, the poem glows with radiance and ends on a note of confidence and hope. But it would be only natural to ask: is it more than another telling of a story already well known?

In one of his essays, the poet has, appropriately enough, touched on this point. "Whoever", he says, "dares make use of an old story that has already been told skilfully in noble language should have some new meaning to put into the old story or a new way of saying it." Elsewhere he says that he had made use of some of the legends of the past to set forth some of his experiences of life as he had felt it. Furthermore he believed "that these ancient myths and legends are unequalled for conveying the pattern of men's reactions and thoughts at their deepest, even unconscious levels". And I think it can be shown that his YMADAWIAD ARTHUR has a significance beyond the pleasure derived from the unfolding of the narrative.

I believe that certain aspects of the story as told here can be interpreted symbolically. Bedwyr instinctively wants to keep the sword: there was a tradition and a profound common belief that a country could not survive without powerful arms to protect it. Bedwyr tries to rationalise his reluctance to cast the sword away and hides it in a dark cave, as one tries to avoid carrying out an unpleasant task by trying to forget it. But Arthur, who knows the pattern of the past and the future, insists that the sword must go back to the lake whence it came. And when Arthur explains to Bedwyr why he cannot accompany his master to Afallon, and also promises to return, we are inevitably made to think that there is here perhaps more than a parallel to such passages as this from the Scriptures:

Yet a little while am I with you, and then I go . . . and where I am thither ye cannot come (John 7, 33-34).

Like the disciples, Bedwyr, in his perplexity, has to return to the struggle even though he is now alone, and must await the return of his leader. Further, Arthur is conceived in one way on the pattern of the Suffering Servant, in another, a Messiah, and his disappearance and subsequent promise of a return in glory are not without some similarity to the teaching in the Gospel.

Then let us take the verses quoted above, which describe the isle of Afallon. Not only is it the home of all that the poet could wish for in a "pleasant land" of his dreams and imagination but the verses also give expression to the hopes and aspirations of the CYMRU FYDD *(The Wales of the Future)* political and cultural movement of the years around the turn of the century. It is true that most of these elements are to be found in the original story but I think that the poet has given them particular prominence because they had a special significance for him at that time, even though, as he put it, their appeal was perhaps only at an unconscious level.

Earlier in this essay I said that this poem marks a new era in the history of Welsh poetry. For most of the previous century Welsh poets in their odes and lyrics had been preoccupied with moral and Biblical, and even historical subjects and events—particularly those of a catastrophic nature. It was only natural that they should be written in Scriptural language and in the abstract terms and idioms of moral treatises. In addition, these diffuse and uninspired poems made use of a great variety of the verse forms of the *cynghanedd* metres with little regard for any artistic or elegant pattern. But in his ode T. Gwynn Jones concentrated on telling the story, limiting himself to three simple verse forms and using the seven-syllable *cywydd* rhymed-couplet mainly for the narrative passages. This use of the *cywydd* line for narrative purposes was, in some respects, revolutionary for it was a metre used originally centuries ago, for love poems, elegies and contemplative subjects. In addition, T. Gwynn Jones made it the vehicle of the dialogue between Bedwyr and Arthur about disposing of the sword, Caledfwlch. And in all this it was handled with a mastery that one would previously have thought impossible. Together with this we have a break with the traditional vocabulary. As the subject matter had its origin in the world of medieval romance, the poet made extensive use of terms and phrases found in the Welsh versions of those romances and in the poetry of the bards in late medieval times. This gave the poem a freshness and an appeal the like of which no poem had had for a long time. This appeal was mainly to the young, particularly those who were reading Welsh in college or university: their linguistic training made it possible for them to appreciate its style and its form. (Twenty-five years later, in a new collection of his poems for publication, the poet revised its language drastically in parts, substituting more modern and current verbal and other forms for the many archaisms in the original poem.)

Wordsworth in his *Preface* to the Lyrical Ballads says that "every great and original writer, in proportion as he is great and original, must create the taste by which he is to be relished". And this is what the poetry of T. Gwynn Jones did. Soon people realised that the idiom of this poetry was not a novel way of writing the language but indeed a return to the true and traditional idiom as it was still spoken and as it had always been written before it had been corrupted in imitation of English idiom by most of the leading writers of the nineteenth century. As a result, literary men found themselves showing their appreciation of this ode by imitating it and starting a new tradition where the *cynghanedd* metres and the idiom of the language were treated with a respect and devotion that had been lacking in Welsh poetry for generations.

Seven years later in the 1909 National Eisteddfod, the poet again found a subject to his liking. The set theme for the ode, or *awdl,* in *cynghanedd* was Gwlad y Bryniau, which can be translated as *The Land of Hills*. As might be expected, the poet took this to be the land of Wales, and presents us in his ode with four different aspects or impressions of life in the land, romantic in conception and evocative in its idiom and vocabulary.

In the first part we are given a glimpse of a party of maidens dancing like fairies in a forest clearing in the moonlight. One, the fairest of them all, sings a plaintive song describing how in this fair isle they had seen better days; their ancestors had been living in peace, but when fair-haired invaders had come from across the sea, they had been forced to find refuge in these mountain recesses and impenetrable forests.

In the second section, headed *War,* we are presented with another aspect: we hear sounds as of an army getting ready for battle; two armies near a fortified town are approaching each other across a valley with the sun shining on their armour. A fierce battle ensues, the armies being compared to two sea cross currents meeting in full force. But as night approaches, the fury is spent, and stillness reigns except for the cries of ravens and wolves in the valley. A fire is seen on one of the nearby ridges, and in its light the poet sees two figures, one an old man, the other a youth. The older man finds his harp and sings the sad song of the Chieftain's Son and the Maid of the Mountain. The legend tells of the chieftain's son losing his way while out with the hunt. He hears a sweet song coming from the hills, goes in search of it, and finds it is the song sung by a very beautiful maiden. He pursues her and eventually she agrees to be his bride as long as he does not ask about his own land and possessions. Soon his longing gets the better of him and he pleads to be allowed to return for a time to his own land and people. Thereupon she shows him a secret path back to his own country; but on getting there, he is not to be comforted, and pines to return to his loved one. He cannot, however, find his way and dies in the effort; his restless spirit still haunts the hills.

The third section, headed *Romance,* is an idyll; on an autumn afternoon, the poet imagines he comes upon a surpassing fair lady in a glen, and a young man comes to meet her. Then calling the young man Dafydd, the poet gives us a passage in the style of Dafydd ap Gwilym where Dafydd is seen trying to entice the fair lady to abandon her idea of taking the veil and to join him in a service in the woodland "church" where the wine is twice as good as the wine of the gods. She pretends that she is unconvinced, but on further persuasion, the young couple move off in the direction of the woodland.

The last section, entitled *Renaissance,* takes us to an ancient castle, where a harpist delights a big crowd on the lawn with his singing. Then a speaker of great eloquence comes to address the people gathered there. He reminds his hearers of the beauty of their incomparable language; many invaders had threatened its existence from Roman to Norman; but it had survived and indeed had, by its romances and legends, made the Norman captive:

> *Tithau â'th ramant weithion a'i meddwaist,*
> *Oni liwiaist y byd â'th chwedleuon.*

(You, with your romances, eventually made him drunk and thereby coloured the world with your legends.)

The speaker in his peroration declares boldly of the language that despite the insults hurled at it, it will undoubtedly survive:

> *A byw, o'th faeddwyd, dros byth a fyddi.*

And as he finishes his last sentence there is a crash of thunder over the town. He turns to his audience and says: "Hear the cry of our gods." The crowd then rise and sing together; and on scattering, they feel the air charged with music for the rest of the evening; for the spirit of this nation is invincible.

Such, very sketchily, is the content of the ode. It can be argued that there is an apparent lack of coherence between the four sections, but in itself each section sounds convincing. The most memorable part perhaps is the story told of the Chieftain's Son and the Maid of the Mountains, particularly how he was dissatisfied with their happy life together, his wish to return to his previous way of life and then his desperate quest for the paradise he had lost. The poet returned to this subject in another poem soon after writing this ode, and this theme of the 'paradise that has been lost' was to recur time and again in his poetry from now on. The last section also has a significance beyond recording an impression of a gathering on the lawn of an ancient castle. There is no mistaking the implications of the incident with which the ode ends: here we have—actually based on a historical incident—another expression of the hopes and aspirations of individuals and the members of the movement who were concerned with independence for Wales and respect and status for the language.

After this second triumph in the National Eisteddfod T. Gwynn Jones came to be acclaimed the leading poet of his generation as author of odes in the *cynghanedd* metres. As already stated, his language and style had, in the words of Wordsworth quoted above, "created the taste by which he was relished"; indeed, such was the admiration for his work that the language and idiom of his poetry were being extensively imitated not only in *cynghanedd* odes but in the longer free metre eisteddfod poems.

During this period the poet had not confined his poetic efforts to the eisteddfod ode. In 1910 he published a substantial volume of poetry— "Ymadawiad Arthur and Other Poems". This contained his 1902 ode and a wealth of miscellaneous poems including some narrative or ballad verse of a romantic nature. There were also some pieces of translation from Horace, but there are two very important pieces: Y NEF A FU *(The Heaven that was)*, a poem in the Fitzgerald Omar Khayyâm verse form in which the poet regrets the passing of the state of bliss of his innocent childhood:

> *Nid rhyfedd mwyach na ddaw imi'r nef*
> *A gollais gynt, er llawer truan lef;*
> *Yn ôl cyweirio 'ngwely lle yr wyf,*
> *Nid oes i mi ond gorwedd arno ef.*

(It is no wonder now that I cannot attain to the heaven I once lost, despite my frequent cries. As I have prepared for myself a bed where I now am, I have no alternative but to lie on it.)

Another outstanding poem of this period is a compact one in the *cywydd* metre; in it he describes a journey he and a great friend of his, W. J. Gruffydd, made presumably on foot like two pilgrims from Bangor on a fine Sunday morning in May 1906 to visit the ruins of the priory of Penmon near Beaumaris on the coast of Anglesey. He describes the flowers by the roadside on the way there as well as a seagull in flight and a crane they noticed on a rock in the Menai Straits; then the ruins of the fine doorway, the fish pond and the well of drinking water and the pigeon house. These were still to be seen in the ruins but he then imagines he can hear the bells and the organ, together with the sound of the monks singing vespers in Latin as they did in the distant past. But the charm is broken; only the ruins remain and they will never be able to see the monks who lived there. The appeal of this poem lies in its restrained language, the visual images it presents, and though we are asked to imagine that we can hear the monks chanting their Latin, the regret at the end is that we will not be able to see them. The works of nature survive, but the works of man, even Latin, pass away. It is a good example of one of the main features of some of his best poetry—the ability to describe the 'outside of things', showing here in classical form a romantic approach to his theme.

Now that he was being acclaimed as one of the leading poets of his day he gave up competing for eisteddfod prizes. He had also by this time (1909) left the world of journalism and had moved to Aberystwyth to work in the newly established National Library. And it was at this time that he composed the delightful poem entitled TÍR NA N-ÓG (*The Land of the Ever Young*). He had dealt with the theme briefly in the song of the Chieftain's Son in GWLAD Y BRYNIAU—the young man who turned his back on the paradise he had found with his loved one because he could not forget the call of his own land and people. This time the poet took an old Irish legend and wrote it in full *cynghanedd* metres as a kind of libretto for an opera. The story goes like this:

Osian, a young poet, has been out hunting with his companions, and on the way home meets Nia of the Golden Hair, daughter of the King of Tír na n-Óg. They fall in love and she takes him with her back to her island home off the coast of Ireland. They live there in perfect bliss for a long time. But despite this care-free existence Osian still remembers his home, his hounds and his companions on the isle of Rathlîn, and his longing to return overwhelms him. The life in Tír na n-Óg is far too perfect to keep its hold on him:

> *O! fwynaf Ynys Ienctyd,*
> *Ai rhy ddi-fai dy hardd fyd*
> *I ddal anesmwyth galon*
> *Dyn o hyd a denu hon?*

(Oh island of the ever young, is your state of bliss too flawless to keep its hold on the heart of man?)

He pines to return to see his old home, and despite warnings from Nia and her attendants that time will catch up with him if he touches the ground there, his wish to return is irresistible and he insists on going on a visit to his native land. There he finds the place in ruins; men—mere dwarfs compared with the men of his day—are attempting to rebuild his home but they find the stones too big and heavy for them to handle. Osian, riding his horse, offers to place these stones for them if given in a golden bowl some of the wine they used to drink in his day. After drinking the wine he lifts the heavy stone, but as he does so the saddle girdle snaps and he falls to the ground. On being picked up he is found to have aged, and instantly dies. Such is the tragic end of Osian.

This short play—for it can and has been produced as a play and a splendid spectacle—shows the poet's fine taste and metrical and verbal skill. The three scenes are short, and the dialogue brief, with no lengthy speeches or descriptions, but with delightful lyrics for the lovers in both the first and second scene.

In essence the story—like the one about *Mab y Pennaeth* in the second part of GWLAD Y BRYNIAU— is an expression of man's unceasing quest for happiness and satisfaction, but, when he thinks he has found it, he is still not satisfied. Woman's needs are also different from man's: Nia is contented and satisfied but Osian is uneasy and unsettled. We have the same point made in the story of Diarmuid and Grainne: Diarmuid's love is enough for Grainne but he is uneasy and longs for the fellowship of Fionn and his other companions. Furthermore, Osian is also a poet, and on his return to his homeland, deplores its sad state. This can be interpreted as the literary tradition which needs rebuilding but which can only be done with the material from the ruins of the old: in other words, the literary revival must be rooted in the true traditional modes of the language and the literary forms. One can even go further and suggest that there can be no total return to the past; only death lies that way. And it was this that the poet had attempted and accomplished in this early but important period in his literary career.

In the space of a short essay like this it would be folly to try to touch upon the great number of shorter poems that are found in the 1910 collection. As stated above, he had now moved to Aberystwyth and had taken up a different kind of work. But back in 1905 he had contracted a stubborn cold, and a doctor advised him to spend the winter in a warmer and drier climate. As a result of arrangements made for him through the kindness and generosity of some friends he was able to go by sea to Egypt for the winter of that year, and after several months there he returned in the Spring very much improved in health. The result of this 'exile' was a small volume of prose entitled Y MÔR CANOLDIR A'R AIFFT *(The Mediterranean Sea and Egypt)*—which was published in book form in 1912. In substance it consists of an edited form of the letters he had written weekly to his wife during the voyage out and the time he spent in Egypt.

In its twenty-seven short chapters the author gives us his impressions of the people he met on his travels and in various *pensions* where he stayed in Egypt. This period in his life, though one of great anxiety for him and for his family and friends, gave him the leisure—enforced, admittedly—to read widely, to think over many things, and also an opportunity to practise his knowledge of foreign languages in the company of the mixed nationalities in the various *pensions*. These 'impressions' that he has recorded do not pretend to be profound studies of life in the Middle East, but they do reveal a man of very wide sympathies ready to try to understand other religions and ways of life, and particularly interested in all sorts of people and their ideas and customs in all kinds of places. In addition it is written in an easy and unobtrusive literary style with no attempt at 'fine' writing.

But there are passages in this volume which are echoed elsewhere in his writings. There is one passage in particular which is of interest to students of his literary style, the passage where he describes the pyramid region:

The golden light one finds in the East when the sun is about to set was like a flood over [the great pyramid at Ghizeh], an amber haze, as if the sky had 'set' into a long lake of honey and one was looking and seeing things through it. To the east the sky is rose-coloured. Westward it is the colour of honey, the earth looking as if it were a denser layer of the same thing . . . It was like a scene from a dream, or like the view from parts of Snowdonia over Menai and Anglesey when the sun on a summer evening sets into clouds which look like mountains and valleys, forests and castles.

There is, perhaps, especially in translation, nothing remarkable in this; but as he himself has stated somewhere that he never in his poetry described any scenery or landscape which he had not himself witnessed, I think that it was a picture of what he describes above that he had in mind when composing the opening lines of the poem BROSELIAWND and also the scene of an 'incomparable land' that we are given in the last section of MADOG.

THOMAS GWYNN JONES

As recorded above, we know that the poet, by about 1910 had spent nearly twenty years in the world of weekly newspapers in various towns, and though he had now taken up work which meant more regular hours, he was by no means idle. Soon after coming to Aberystwyth he started lecturing to extra-mural classes arranged by the University College. He also found himself attracted to academic studies and in THE TRANSACTIONS OF THE CYMMRODORION SOCIETY for 1913-14 he published, in English, under the title of BARDISM AND ROMANCE, a scholarly study of the old bardic traditions and of the patterns of our early poetry. For this study he was granted a Master's degree of the University and in the same year joined the staff of the Welsh Department in the College. In addition to exacting work of this nature, he was engaged at the same time on two biographies, one of Emrys ap Iwan which appeared in 1912 and another of Thomas Gee which appeared in the following year. And no estimate of the work of Thomas Gwynn Jones would be anywhere near a fair one without mention of these two works.

Emrys ap Iwan, or the Reverend Robert Ambrose Jones, a Calvinistic Methodist minister who had spent most of his time in ministries in Denbighshire, had died in 1905. He had been writing extensively and vigorously in the press for a period of over thirty years under the name Emrys ap Iwan. Biographies of denominational worthies were very numerous in this period, but this one of Emrys was a biography with a difference, for the subject and the biographer were not on the usual pattern. Emrys, after leaving the theological college at Bala had spent some years in Switzerland teaching English in a school there, and of course learning French and German. He was thus a man of very wide culture and sympathies. When he returned to Wales and became a candidate for the ministry, obstacles were raised to ordaining him as he had vigorously attacked in the press the policy of some leaders of the denomination in promoting the establishment of English chapels in many totally Welsh towns. In addition Emrys had criticised the stilted and magniloquent contemporary way of writing Welsh practised by many authors in imitation of certain English styles. He had also dared to refuse to give evidence as a witness in English in a court of law in his native Denbighshire, and as a result, when his protest had been reported in the daily newspapers, Emrys was denounced, insulted and reviled for this stand both in the English and Welsh press and in scores of anonymous letters. He was an accomplished essayist and journalist able to write his native language with grace and precision.

T. Gwynn Jones had worked with Emrys ap Iwan on the staff of the weekly radical Y FANER in Denbigh, and the older man had been a kind of teacher and mentor for the young writer for many years. T. Gwynn Jones had therefore an exceptionally colourful and controversial subject for his book, a rare figure whom he admired for his non-conformity and the way he had returned to challenge the mandarins of his own denomination. He was also a man of scholarly and literary sympathies; above all he had stood for integrity in writing his native language, and had made a bold effort to have it respected enough to be made the medium of instruction in the schools.

In his preface to this biography the author tells us:

I have attempted, as far as the material was available to me, to let him tell his own story, knowing that neither I nor anyone else can do him the justice which his own writings and letters can give him.

As Emrys ap Iwan had been a prolific writer in the weekly and periodical press there was plenty of documentary evidence for his biographer to work on. The result is a sober and well documented account of Emrys ap Iwan's many sided interests and sympathies, written certainly by an admirer, and that in a direct and unpretentious idiom making it one of the outstanding biographies in the language.

Within a year Gwynn Jones had, in May 1913, produced another biography, that of Thomas Gee of Denbigh. His industry must have been immense, for this second one was a study running into six-hundred-and-thirty pages. The task itself was a massive one; the amount of material available for the sixty years of the very active life of Thomas Gee was in itself enormous, and required a vast amount of reading and arranging. In a later chapter of the work, Gwynn Jones wrote:

In this work the intention was to let the speeches, articles, letters and deeds of Thomas Gee show us what sort of man he was and what he did. To set them out in their proper perspective it was necessary to relate the history of Wales for nearly sixty years.

The result is a well documented and comprehensive study of many of the main movements in the political and cultural life of Wales in the Victorian era. Thomas Gee was the proprietor of a printing and publishing house in Denbigh, and the editor of the widely read radical and liberal Welsh weekly called Y FANER or BANER AC AMSERAU CYMRU. As editor and an influential politician Thomas Gee concerned himself with such movements as elementary and higher education, in particular the founding of Aberystwyth College with its initial difficulties and internal tensions; the Tithe War of the eighties, the Home Rule movement, Temperance, Church Disestablishment and the work of the Land Commission together with the constantly changing pattern of Welsh political life. Thomas Gee, though a staunch Calvinistic Methodist, was an enlightened radical and Liberal in politics, and the young poet had spent the major part of five years in his employ as one of the sub-editors of Y FANER. "I was privileged to know Mr Gee well", he says in his preface to the work, "when he was an old man and I a young one." The young protégé had a profound admiration for the "grand old man" of Welsh public life, for his liberal outlook and for the firm but restrained way he had of furthering his views and promoting causes he deemed worthy of support.

In reading this work one cannot but marvel at the skill which went into summarising and translating scores of passages from press reports of public and parliamentary speeches and policy statements or commission reports, all of which has been accomplished in a masterly way, the style being fluent and the transition from narrative to reported speech being smooth and easy. And in a passage in one of the final chapters, where he describes the fine autumn day on which Thomas Gee was buried, after being absorbed for hundreds of pages in the policies and polemics of Victorian Wales, we realise that the author is indeed the poet of YMADAWIAD ARTHUR and MADOG.

As he tells us in the course of these two works, his aim in both was to place these two public figures in their setting and to let their own words and deeds speak for them. No attempt is made to write an "intimate" biography or to subject the two figures to some kind of psychological analysis by trying to probe into their private motives or hidden frustrations (if any!) or to suggest that they were markedly different people in private from what they appeared in public.

By this time Gwynn Jones had become a leading figure in the literary life of Wales. After nineteen years from the age of nineteen to thirty-eight as a hard working journalist he had left the world of a newspaperman and had now been appointed to the post of a full-time lecturer in a University College, and this through his own effort, for he had not had any kind of formal higher education. He was one of the acknowledged masters in the field of poetry, and had two substantial volumes to his name; he had also made an important contribution to scholarship in his volume on

BARDISM AND ROMANCE, and his two volumes of biography were impressive studies of the lives of two very important persons in the life of Wales in the latter half of the previous century. He also still made valuable contributions to Welsh periodicals as well as to the monthly English language review THE WELSH OUTLOOK.

It was at this time that he wrote his next important long poem Y GYNNEDDF GOLL *(The Lost Sense)*. It is conceived in a romantic setting but it reflects the poet's dissatisfaction with the way the world was going and in particular his own uncertainty in the world of religious belief. It is not written in one of the strict *cynghanedd* metres, but it is interesting to note that as the poem proceeds, the poet finds, as it were, that he is making more and more regular use of *cynghanedd,* this fact showing that he was by this time so much at home in the use of *cynghanedd* that he almost found it difficult not to use it. The argument runs briefly as follows:

The poet, having retreated on a fine summer's day to the noble ruins of Strata Florida, has a dream, and in it he is approached by a Grey Friar whose tone was gentle but firm. This "monk" tells him of his religious pilgrimage. He had left the "monastery" at its dissolution and had gone to live in the city where he tried to find satisfaction in the study and pursuit of the visual arts, in the study of history, the new humanism and the pursuit of liberty. He then tried to understand what modern science had to say about man's destiny but there was no comfort or satisfaction in this line of thought, which seemed to suggest that the world would end in total disintegration.

But despite all the claims of science and the prophets of progress, man remained a cruel and selfish being, unable to master his own passions; and life was only made tolerable by living it according to some set and petty rules. So the monk had turned his back on formal religion and the academies of learning and had wandered in storm and rain until he came to the ruins of Strata Florida. He realised that here had been the refuge of his ancestors when the faith of Christ had flourished before man had tried to make himself the master of the universe; here art had been made to serve a higher purpose than for its own sake. He asked if Christ was still abroad in this "faith-less" world, or was he still buried in his grave. Was the cry on the Cross a cry in vain as also the suffering? Who would not exchange all knowledge for a moment of the peace of the Faith that was no longer with us? He believed he could see the image of the Cross on the floor; his fear left him, and the storm in his soul subsided. He regretted that he had not seen this clear light to lead him at the beginning of his search, though his journeyings in the world outside were not altogether unpleasant; yet the pain and the grief had been a burden, and the effort to find peace of mind in the world had been a vain search.

The poet then leaves the place knowing not if what he had heard in the ruins was true; but he had realised that to some had been given the knowledge that the grave is not the end of living, or as he put it in a typical epigrammatic way:

Ond gwn roi'r ddawn a ŵyr
I rai, nad dibyn bedd yw eithaf diben byw.

(For I realised that to some had been given the gift of knowing that the edge of the grave is not the final purpose of life.)

There is no need to elaborate on the meaning of the symbolism used here: the poet is trying to say as in his description of the Chieftain's Son and Osian's quest in *Tír na n-Óg* that man is forever seeking the ideal life: in the two former poems this lost paradise is situated outside the world of men but in this poem it is presumably to be found in the past—in the Age of the Faith, before man's inquisitiveness broke through the confines of that neatly ordered world. This is a theme that will recur in many of the poems that we shall deal with later on.

By this time, in 1914, war had caused many of the "lights to go out all over Europe". Because of the many added responsibilities of his work in the University we find but a few poems for the first part of the war period. Then suddenly in 1917 a new long poem of three-hundred-and-fifty lines appeared under the title MADOG. Most people have heard the legend about this supposed son of Owain Gwynedd who had sailed westwards across the Atlantic in the twelfth century and had landed in America. There he had settled, and by mixing with an Indian tribe, had founded a colony of Welsh-speaking American Indians. The poet Robert Southey had composed a long poem on the subject in 1805, and had given great prominence to the settlement in America. Then in a very long Welsh poem of about two thousand lines the poet Cadvan had told the same kind of story for a competition in the National Eisteddfod of 1884. Neither of these had attempted anything beyond a full narrative of the legend.

T. Gwynn Jones, on the other hand, made use of the story to embody his reaction to the war being waged in Europe in those years. He tells us in a note which he wrote at the end of the text of MADOG on the manuscript of the Gregynog edition of 1926 of his CANIADAU: "This [poem] was written as some sort of an escape from the horrors of the period. It does not appear that anyone realised it at the time!" This statement shows that the poet was not interested in the theme just as a story to tell; on the other hand he felt he could not convey his reaction in a short poem or a series of lyrics; he felt he wanted a story to give unity to his theme, thereby putting into practice some advice that he had given from time to time when adjudicating in eisteddfodau:

A story has value in any kind of long poem to prevent it merely repeating the one theme as is sometimes done in music; it also makes it into a single whole rather than a series of variations.

The question now arose what kind of metre he should use. He had become convinced that many of the strict *cynghanedd* verse forms of the traditional odes were too inflexible and exacting, but that *cynghanedd* itself was more akin to the genius of the language than rhyme. It so happened also that just before the war Sir John Rhŷs, one of the foremost Celtic scholars of the age, had propounded a theory that the four-line

Welsh *englyn* verse form was ultimately derived from an accented late Latin form of the classical elegiac couplet. Without necessarily accepting this interesting theory, Gwynn Jones was intrigued by it, and conceived the idea of using the *englyn* as the unit of his new poem. It was written as two long lines, one of sixteen syllables and the other of fourteen, each line having six stressed syllables, the stresses as in all *cynghanedd* verse, coming where the speech rhythm and sense demand it; but the end rhyme of the traditional *englyn* was discarded. Furthermore, as the hero of the poem was to be a legendary character of near heroic proportions it was only fitting that the tale should be told in a metre which seemed to have a traditional connection with classical heroic poetry.

The story of the poem can be given in outline like this:

It is evening with a gentle breeze moaning in the bushes and reeds on the banks of the river Menai, and Madog, the son of Owain, Prince of Gwynedd, is wandering there in an uneasy mood. Owain, the father, is dead, and lies buried in the cathedral church at Bangor. His life had been a stormy one, and Madog had been the captain of his fleet. Madog, who was never at peace except when he was afloat then recalls Mabon, the Priest, who had been his mentor in his young days, and is sad that he had not in his youth listened to Mabon's advice. He would be glad indeed to meet his old teacher again. Then out of the gathering darkness he hears a voice calling him by name and on investigating finds Mabon, who receives him and blesses him as he kneels before him. Madog addresses him as his father, and asks his forgiveness; in reply Mabon requests him to tell him what it is that worries him, for he still loves him as a son, and on his many wanderings he has constantly prayed God that Madog should be restored to him.

But Madog, having confessed to many a savage deed in the name of a love for his country, asks the Priest if there is any more "a God in heaven; has he not perished?"

"Dywed, O dad", medd Madog, "O dad, a oes Duw yn y nefoedd?
Onid aeth Duw i'r annuw, O dad, oni threngodd Duw?"

Mabon answers him firmly that there can be no doubt on this point:

"Duw", medd y llall, "ni adawodd ei nef na'i ofal amdanom,
Duw a luniodd ein daear, Duw o'i thrueni a'i dwg;
Byr yw ein dyddiau, fel barrug y ciliant rhag heulwen y bore,
Mil o flynyddoedd fel undydd sydd yn ei hanes Ef . . ."

(God, answered the other, has not left his heaven nor left off caring for us; he formed the earth, and he will redeem it from its misery; our days are short and they fade away like dew before the morning sunshine, and a thousand years are as a mere day in his time . . .)

The Priest then goes on to tell of his own spiritual pilgrimage; how on one of the Crusades he had seen violence done in the name of Jesus. He had at first accepted the teachings of St Bernard in matters of unbelief but later Abelard had shaken those views, and Abelard's words were indeed as refreshing as the breezes of spring. Eventually Mabon restores to Madog his faith.

*Diwedd a ddaeth i'r duwiau, a diwedd i'r duwiau ddaw eto,
Duw, er hynny un diwedd byth yn ei hanes ni bydd.*

(Gods have perished in the past, and an end will come to gods again; but God will never cease to exist.)

Despite Madog's uncertainty as to the value of confessing Christ, Mabon reassures him and states that men have not given up confessing their allegiance to Christ and his Cross. He had seen the place where Christ was crucified for us and also the grave where he lay, but He is with us ever, despite the grave:

*"Tyfed y byd fel y tyfo, boed ef na bo dim nas gwypo,
Dyn ni chyfodir a dynno ddim o'i wirionedd Ef."*

(Let the world develop as it will, and let there be nothing that it does not know, there never will be a man who can undermine His truth in any way or form.)

Thus assured, Madog invites his old teacher to go with him to Gwenan Gorn, his flagship, lying at anchor at Aber Menai. Madog tells him that this ship is his retreat, the cradle of his imagination, the handmaid of all his longings and his means of escape into freedom.

The second section opens with the break of dawn on a sunny day, with Madog on board his ship near his fleet off Aber Menai. The man on look-out espies a fleet of ships approaching from the west, and at Madog's command they put out to sea to investigate. The other ships turn and make for the Holyhead headland with Madog and his men in swift pursuit, all of them roused by the prospect of a battle. On closing in on the "invaders" Madog finds that it is the fleet of his brother Hywel, a fleet he had raised in Ireland to try to regain control of Gwynedd which their brother Dafydd had usurped when Hywel was away in Ireland claiming his inheritance there. Madog tries to pacify Hywel but he will not submit to the traitor Dafydd, and refuses to acknowledge him. Madog decides not to interfere when Hywel orders his men to try to land on the Anglesey shore. But Dafydd's troops are there to prevent the landing, and the battle rages indecisively for a long time until at last a stray arrow strikes Hywel and wounds him in the heart. With their leader mortally wounded the men of Ireland panic and retreat over the sea. This section ends with a description of the death of Hywel, Prince of Gwynedd, the poet who had sung of the many beauties of nature—the snow and the dawn, the sea-shore and the gleam of sunshine on the sea.

Truan y troai Hywel ei olwg wrth alwad y Mynach,
Ofer y gwingodd ei wefus—mud ydoedd honno mwy;
Cododd y meddwl cayedig i'w legach lygad yn ddeigryn
Arhosodd fel gem o risial tawdd wrth yr amrant hir,
Yna disgynnodd hyd wyneb Hywel, a chaeodd yr amrant,
Ias ag uchenaid isel, a dim lle bu'r nwydau oll.

(Hywel turned his face in pain at the call of the Priest; his lip trembled in vain for it had lost the power of speech; the imprisoned thought rose to his tired eyes as a tear which clung to his eyelid; then it rolled down over Hywel's face, and the eyelid shut, then just a shiver and a weak sigh and there is nothing left where all those passions had been!)

In the third section it is again night, and Madog and Mabon are together. Hywel's death has moved Madog, and he wants to know why men should behave like this, why they cheat and deceive one another and resort to war to settle their differences, thus living in the shackles of futile and obsolete customs and practices. Had not Mabon at one time said there was a land somewhere in the far reaches of the sea where one could escape from the troubles of war and the dissensions and feuds that were the curse of human life? Mabon replies that there is such a place on an island very much as described in Irish legends. Many brave men had sought it and one fair maiden had described it like this:

"Ynys", medd hi, "sydd ynghanol môr y gorllewin maith;
Prydferth wanegau'n chwerthin ar dawel aur dywod ei glannau,
Haul drwy'r ewyn yn eilio rhwyd fel o saffir a rhos;
Gwâr ar ddyffryn Gwynarian, di-fâr yw difyrrwch y cedyrn,
Ir trwy yr oesau yr erys y fro, dan ei blodau'n frith;
Yno, tragywydd trig ieuanc, galar nag wylo ni ddyfydd,
Fyth, i'r ynys gyfoethog, briw ni bydd yno na brad."

(There is an isle far out in the west where bright waves break on its golden sands, and the sunshine through the wave crests makes patterns of rose and of sapphire. The mighty men who dwell on the island of Gwynarian delight themselves in peace without malice, while the landscape is forever green and covered with flowers. There all men remain forever young, and neither grief nor sorrow, pain nor deceit are ever to be found on this pleasant island.)

Madog is delighted at the prospect of going to look for this place over the sea; he is never more at peace than when sailing, and he remembers how he had no patience with the flattery of poets at his father's court. He will go on this quest and acknowledge the Christ again as the one who had stilled the storm on the sea—He who was the son of the Queen of the Ocean.

In the fourth and last section it is dawn on a spring morning, and just outside Menai are ten ships with three hundred men on board, ready to set out with Madog as their leader. Later there is a masterly description of a sunset over the western sea, the whole cloud pattern forming a picture of an "incomparable land"; but despite its beauty it was unattainable for there was no substance in all this grandeur. The ships are now well out at sea sailing in fine weather where all is quiet and delightful:

Diwyd a hir fu'r mordwyo hyd eigion nas digiai awel,
Haul yr haf ar yr heli, a lloer yr haf ar y lli . . .

(The voyage was long and steady over an ocean undisturbed by the breeze with summer sunshine on the water and a summer moon on the deep.)

But the calm is deceptive; there is a powerful swell in the sea and soon they find themselves in a fierce hurricane, the ensuing storm being in great contrast to the preceding calm. The men know that they are the victims in an unequal struggle, and soon the only ship afloat is Gwenan Gorn, Madog's flagship. Then its rails and masts have gone "like rushes before the storm". The buffeting has loosened the planks and death is rising inch by inch in the hold. Then comes this final passage:

Gair ni lefarwyd ond gŵyrodd Madog, a mud y penlinodd,
Ufudd y plygodd hefyd ei lu yn ei ymyl ef;

Yna cyfododd y Mynach ei law a'i lef tua'r nefoedd,
Arwydd y Grôg a dorrodd, a'i lais a dawelai ofn;
Rhonciodd y llong, a rhyw wancus egni'n ei sugno a'i llyncu,
Trystiodd y tonnau trosti, bwlch ni ddangosai lle bu.

(No word was spoken but Madog approached and knelt in silence with his men beside him. The Priest then raised his arm and his voice to heaven, making the sign of the Cross over them, and his voice calmed their fears. The ship lurched as some mighty force gulped and swallowed it, the waves splashed over it leaving no mark where it had been.)

Perhaps it would be of some value to say something of what this long and important poem has to say. It is fairly obvious that Gwynn Jones is not writing it as history or a mere tale of adventure. To begin with the historian knows of no son of Owain Gwynedd called Madog, but some such legend had been current for several centuries, and many authors like Southey and Cadvan, as stated above, had accepted the tale as history.

In this poem I think it would be right to say that the poet himself is Madog; he is trying to hold on to his values in the turmoil of the 1914-18 war. Like Mabon (and Madog too) in the poem he has found his religious faith shaken in the intellectual and political climate of the beginning of the present century, and the outbreak of war in Europe had shattered men's belief in the inevitability of progress and the vague belief that had taken the place of the old doctrine, the belief, so well expressed by Tennyson, of some

"one far-off divine event
To which the whole creation moves."

When the war did come, truth and justice and the work of the artist were among the first casualties. Hywel, in the poem is a symbol of the artist; we all know, according to the story, that his cause was just and that truth was on his side, and yet, in the fierce battle for power and influence, the innocent and guileless, be their cause just and blameless, will be the first to be sacrificed in war. The poet had seen this happen in the war years when people who insisted on telling the truth had to be made to keep silent and when false and misleading propaganda flourished in newspapers and periodicals. And the masterly description of the end of Hywel presents us with one of the most poignant scenes in the whole of our literature: the many skills and delights of Hywel the poet in his lifetime are contrasted with the stark nothingness when life in the form of a tear had ebbed out of him.

Mabon, the Priest (as I have called him) is undoubtedly the Christian faith disguised as a "monk" in this tale with a medieval setting. He had been Madog's mentor, and Madog had turned his back on the teachings he had had in his youth; but now he once again yearns for comfort and succour from his old teacher. Mabon himself is not really the medieval monk but a twentieth century Christian who in his time has had to cope with doubt and unbelief, but who has surmounted his difficulties and returned to the fold; he is however not too dogmatic in his beliefs for he is prepared to receive Madog back to his confidence without his having to submit to the fullest discipline of the church. His presence and his blessing are a source of strength and courage to Madog and his men in all their tribulations, as the following line, coming twice in the last section shows:

Mabon mor fwyn ei wyneb, Dduw! onid tawel oedd ef!

(Mabon's face is calm; God, how serene he is!)

And in their last ordeal, in the face of inevitable death, his voice rings full of comfort above the raging storm.

Madog is of course the poet himself: his most valuable asset is his ship, that is, his imagination; with this he could leave his miserable and disappointing surroundings and strike out for the pleasant and delightful island in the far reaches of the ocean as described by Mabon. He is the adventurer who strikes out for a newer world when overwhelmed by this one. But ironically, his ship fails to take him to the land of his imagination; the storms of this cruel world are too much for it.

How is one to interpret the end which Madog and his followers meet? Is it an ignominious failure, a final realisation that the land they were making for, and of which they had had a glimpse before leaving this country, that this land in the final analysis was as insubstantial as the clouds in the western sky? And is not this what one would expect of people who refuse to face realities but try to escape to a world created in their own imagination? Or, again, is Madog the fearless adventurer who shows in his daring that the only thing worth doing is to follow the vision granted one in this world?

Much more has, and could be written on this kind of symbolism, but like most great works of art, it can be enjoyed in and for itself. It is, undoubtedly the expression of the poet's experience in a difficult period for him and artists like him. It is conceived on a grand scale and sustained by a dignified vocabulary and style, and in reading it one comes across passages which are manifestly symbolical, others prodigally lyrical mingled with passages like the one describing the death of Hywel, or the final catastrophe at sea, which are impressively heroic.

When the war was over and conditions began to return to normal, T. Gwynn Jones was appointed to the newly created Chair of Welsh Literature at the University College in Aberystwyth. The responsibilities attached to forming a new department together with a great increase in the number of students in all departments entailed increased teaching time with the result that for some time he produced no new major work. But soon, by the early twenties, we find him active—under a pseudonym "G"—as the author of two light novels. For years he had been critical of the attitude of Welsh poets to their craft, and also of the treatment of poets by the public. In a volume of short stories BRETHYN CARTREF ("Home-spun") that he had published in 1913 he tells the pathetic story of an absent minded shop-assistant who was persuaded by his colleagues that he had the makings of a poet. In devious ways they convinced him, and he was soon trying to get his work published in the local press. His personality changed and he grew his hair long to fit the popular idea of a poet. But when he found that some poem that he had worked hard to fashion into a masterpiece had been rejected and thrown into the fire he realised his folly, had his hair cut, succeeded in business and became a Justice of the Peace.

T. Gwynn Jones had also earlier in his career written a poem about Y BARDD (published in the 1910 collection of his works), and in this poem he had tried to show his conception of the genuine poet, a highly romantic view, admittedly, but in essence expressing his idea of the role of a poet. But here again the poet is disillusioned, fate has separated him from his youthful ideals, poems have remained unwritten and he loses sight of the visions he used to have. And there is one phrase in this poem which expresses in a few words the whole attitude of T. Gwynn Jones to his craft as a poet, when he states that the young poet he describes had bestowed his whole intense love on the language—*rhoddes draserch ar yr iaith.*

But experience over many years in the newspaper world had shown him that the ruses and subterfuges of would-be "poets" to get their work published and to win recognition by carrying off the prizes at local eisteddfodau were many and strange to believe, and he set about telling the story of one such aspirant in a novel entitled sarcastically JOHN HOMER. It is a short tale of about a hundred pages mostly broad and sparkling farce with sad undertones. It tells of the ambition of a man who was a very competent tailor in his village, but who had an urge to become a poet and thereby hoped to bring ridicule on the local postman, his rival in the same field. But he is remorselessly caught in his own net, and in the end both have to abandon their grand schemes and revert in humility to the craft they are masters of. It is a hilarious but not cruel satire on one aspect of life in Wales at the beginning of this century.

His other novel—LONA—also written under the pseudonym "G"—is of a very different calibre. This is an attempt—in a romantic medium—to show the impact of new ideas in the sphere of religious beliefs and politics and social customs on the Non-conformist establishment of the time. This kind of work was being done by the dramatists J. O. Francis and D. T. Davies and others through the medium of the theatre, but they all had the same thing more or less in common, namely that their plays were set in the parlours and kitchens of their chapel-going characters, and whenever there was mention of the land-owning class they were objects of ridicule and contempt.

Briefly the story runs something like this:

Merfyn Owen, a young theological student, has just brilliantly completed his academic course, and decides to accept a "call" to a chapel in a small seaside town called Minfor. There he soon comes up against people who, the author says, "were not troubled in any way by the intellectual questions and problems of the age". In addition he befriends a young girl who lives with her parents in a remote country cottage, and who are Catholics. She spends most of her time wandering over the countryside or bathing in the sea, and is treated by the townspeople as if she were one of the gypsies. Merfyn also comes to know a Miss Vaughan, the middle-aged daughter of the local country house, and we find that the latter looks upon Lona, the wild and unschooled country girl from the remote cottage as a rival for the affections of Merfyn Owen. Eventually, after her parents' death and a meeting with Miss Vaughan in which the latter says some cruel things to her, Lona disappears without leaving a trace. But by a strange coincidence Merfyn meets her again as a nurse in a hospital where he had to be treated after a slight accident, and the issue is no longer in doubt.

A romantic enough tale, it might be said, and so from one point of view it is. But there are serious undertones, not least an attempt to treat characters such as Lona and Miss Vaughan as human beings. Lona has her own charm and intelligence and is not just romantically passionate; Miss Vaughan is something other than the daughter of the local squire with a passion for hunting and horses: indeed there is a very touching description of her: Merfyn found her "an amusing companion; if he could only forget the face long enough to know the person behind it. The eye is a hard master: it leaves no chance for the other senses." The same can be said of the attitude to the chapel elders: they are treated as men of mixed motives and not praised as paragons or ridiculed as mere agents of evil. People and their ideas are treated seriously: gypsies, strangers, country-house dwellers and Catholics are treated with genuine sympathy, not disparaged, as in much of the social and literary writings of the time in Wales.

A further attraction of the novel is the smooth and easy flow of the language, never drawing attention to itself. The dialogue keeps very near the colloquial idiom of the language but does not deteriorate into mere dialect. We are used to this kind of writing in the novels of today but we have not realised how much of a feat in many ways it was in those days. Incidentally, a translation of the novel into the Irish language was published in 1955.

Meanwhile the poet in him had not been idle. In the early twenties he wrote the second of two poems with the title EX TENEBRIS *(Out of the Darkness)*, and in this work he tries to record the evolution of man from the primordial mud with "its still mists and minute particles" until he reached a reasonable degree of civilisation. He now experimented with the old eleven syllable line he had used before in another poem, discarding the line end rhymes and substituting for it a series of internal rhymes, reminiscent of the traditional metre of MORFA RHUDDLAN. And when he came to compose the poem GWLAD HUD *(The Land of Magic)*, where he recollects some of the memories of his early childhood, it was necessary to try another metrical pattern. He dealt with this material many years later in a small volume called BRITHGOFION *(Reminiscences)* where he recalls in some detail many of the most impressionistic experiences of his childhood. The material here was fragile and gossamer-like, and the ponderous long line of some of the *cynghanedd* verse forms would have been too restricting. Instead, in order to be able to dart into the far recesses of the memory, he chose a metre which could be "run" quite thinly or compressed with complex forms of *cynghanedd,* in short the resilient eight syllable line of an old variant of a *cywydd* type of metre.

But the poet had another poem forming in his mind, a poem about the place of the artist in society. Here again he was the innovator: he had reached the stage when he could write in the metre of MADOG with almost mechanical facility, and he was no longer satisfied with it except as a vehicle in elegy or epigram. This time he went back to the work of the poets of the time of the princes for his model, taking their ten-syllable line as his norm. He discarded their very elaborate rhyme and other patterns but introduced the regular *cynghanedd* system. This gave him a line having four stressed syllables, but those stressed syllables, as in all true *cynghanedd* poetry, coming where the meaning places them according to the rhythm of the spoken language. In addition there was no verse form, division, as with blank verse in English, coming where sense dictated it.

The title of this new poem is BROSELIAWND, and the author says in an appended note:

Broseliawnd was a legendary forest in Britanny. According to the Romances the wizard Merlin was imprisoned there under the spell of his own magic.

Briefly the poem goes like this: It is a summer afternoon and a kind of mist or haze is spread over the country casting a strange spell over it, much as if the retreat of the gods had been exposed to us: it is a place which knows nothing of need or failure or discord, but is serenely peaceful and quiet.

THOMAS GWYNN JONES

The magician recognises this as the magic land he has longed for and dreamt of, for it satisfies his unquenchable desire for beauty (*nwyd anfarwol y bardd am harddwch*). It had come into existence as a result of a conscious command or "fiat", and for no other purpose than to create a world of beauty.

In the midst of this prospect he sees a land of lakes and extensive forests, and he feels the urge to enter it, debating with himself whether to "bury" himself in this pleasant land and forget the worries of the world, which despite its glossy exterior holds no real peace for the heart of man. Eventually he does turn his back on the world and makes his way into the heart of this forest, where there was an "easy and spell-binding enduring peacefulness".

As can be seen from this brief but inadequate summary an old legend gives substance and coherence to the symbolism. Merlin (*Myrddin* in Welsh) like Madog, has probed into the depths and the limits of human knowledge and has as a result lost the faith of his innocence. But he could not smother the desire for inquiry despite the fact that such questioning brought disappointment. He therefore turned his back on the world of hard and cruel facts and buried himself in a world of his own creation. And the spectacle of the dark grey region which before had inspired him to create a world of beauty became for him a place to hide himself from the disappointment and anguish of living.

In this poem we have an attempt to create a world of splendour and beauty as a contrast to the unsightly world of industry. In this way it differs from previous escapist poems, where the flight was to a region like Afallon or Tír na n-Óg or the "fair island" in MADOG, all of which were assumed to have some sort of existence in the physical world. But in this work, this retreat from the world can come into existence—like the very poem in which it is embodied—at the uttering of a word by the magician. So poetry itself becomes the symbol and the means of a retreat from the harsh realities of mundane existence.

Within three years, in 1925, he produced another major poem (of about 170 lines) under the title of ANATIOMAROS. As his note under the title explains, the name is an old Celtic one meaning "great-of-soul", and the poem tells of a crisis in the life of a clan in Gwernyfed in ancient Gaul, and of the passing of the keeper of the traditions of that clan. It is written in the metre he had used in BROSELIAWND and this gives it a stately rhythm well worthy of its dignified subject.

The story tells us that it is autumn, and the trees heavily laden with fruit in the land of Gwernyfed. It is also time for the clan to leave the Hafod, or summer pastures, and move down to their winter homes in the Hendref. This is an occasion for great excitement, and there is great concern over transporting the communal fire, the gift of the gods, from the highland hearth down to the central hearth in the lowlands and from there to each individual hearth in the Hendref. This fire has not been allowed to go out for many generations, and only pure and undefiled young men and maidens are deemed worthy of the task.

On reaching the lowland home there is a meeting of the elders and druids of the clan to proclaim and expound once more the laws and customs to be observed in this more settled community. Foremost among the members is Anatiomaros, the most respected, the wisest and oldest of them all, so old is he that most of the other elders remember him only as an old man:

> *Efô, rhag angen, fu orau'i gyngor,*
> *A nawdd ei dylwyth yn nyddiau dolur,*
> *Efô o'i gariad a fu gywiraf*
> *O'u tu ym mherygl, Anatiomaros.*

(It was he, Anatiomaros, who in time of need had given the best advice; he in his care for them had been of most value on their side when in danger.)

There is much rejoicing and dancing on this their first night in their winter homes when the fires have been rekindled on the family hearths; for this fire, the gift of the gods, will drive away all the diseases and evils from their dwellings. But the communal fire itself in the middle of the settlement requires to be looked after as has been the custom from time immemorial, and for this first night of winter Anatiomaros undertakes the task as he has done for many years in the past. It is generally believed that by carefully watching the pattern of the clouds forming in the west at sunset the omens for the clan for the coming winter can be discerned. And on this night Anatiomaros perceives a small white cloud appear in the west and spread itself over the western sky in the form of a swan. He dies at his task that night having interpreted this cloud formation as a call for him from the land of the dead.

We are then told how a barge in the form of a stately swan was carved out of one of the forest oaks. The body of Anatiomaros is put on it and a fire kindled beneath it; and just before sunset the barge with the funeral pyre upon it is placed on the river just as the tide in the estuary is turning; the flow of the river and the ebbing tide carry it well out to sea where the strong breeze soon fans the fire to burn the raft and the body; the last we see of it as it moves in the direction of the setting sun is as a burnt-out ember rolling on the waters.

Meanwhile his fellow clansmen have lined the river banks in silence, moving down-stream with the movement of the barge but showing no outward signs of grief or sorrow—for that is how he would wish it—except that as it moves down river and out to sea in flames they chant together:

Ar hynt y meirwon Anatiomaros.

(Anatiomaros is on his way to the abode of the dead.)

But when eventually they see no light or flame on the waters in the west they raise their voices once more in a final lament:

Anatiomaros aeth at y meirwon.

(Anatiomaros has gone to the abode of the dead.)

In this poem T. Gwynn Jones has created his own myth but he has placed it distant in time rather than in space. This glimpse of the life of ancient Gwernyfed is contrasted with the pattern of life in the here and now. As Professor T. J. Morgan has put it in an essay on the work of the poet: "this kind of life was presented as an oasis of leisure and forgetfulness in a wilderness of industry and commerce ... a kind of temporary escape for man's soul from the bustle and sound of the wheels of Progress." The poet also seems to feel that the Welsh and Celtic tradition is showing signs of falling apart and dissolving, and this poem points to such a situation. A heroic picture is given us of the clan's return to the Hendre, and the fire that they bring with them becomes a symbol of the continuity of the tradition and of its essential purity and its excellence. The keeper of this racial tradition is the old druid even as the poet is the guardian of the literary tradition. So we have suggested to us Gwynn Jones's conception of the office of poet, and the way in which the poet or guardian or indeed the whole tradition should pass away, in a noble and dignified way:

Heb air dros wefus, heb rodres ofer.

(Without uttering a word, without any vain show.)

Two of the key words in the poem are *aeddfed* (ripe) and *tân* (fire): the time for Anatiomaros to depart is ripe, like the fruit of the autumn scene. The "fire of the gods" makes life possible for the clan, and it is the fire in the barge together with the salt water of the sea—the two great purifiers—which devoured the remains of Anatiomaros, "the Great of Soul", so that the body does not fall victim to the corruption that is the lot of ordinary mortals. There is no word in the whole poem which is either harsh or sullen, for it glows throughout serenely radiant.

But this is not to say that the poet had shut himself off from the realities of the world around him. We saw in MADOG how dissatisfied he was with the state of the society in which he lived, and in the twenties a strong note of protest and even of satire is found in some of his poems. And when DYCHWELIAD ARTHUR *(The Return of Arthur)* was set as subject of the chair ode in the National Eisteddfod of 1923, T. Gwynn Jones was attracted by the theme and wrote a poem on the subject (not for the competition, of course). The metre used is of his own devising, namely the ten syllable *cynghanedd* line already used in BROSELIAWND but rhymed in couplets.

In the poem he imagines Arthur having returned and come to the scene of the National Eisteddfod disguised as a countryman. The crowd have just been roused to great "national" fervour by a most eloquent speech—*in English,* of course—and everyone is singing lustily the last line of the National Anthem:

> O bydded i'r hen iaith barhau.
>
> *(Long may the ancient language live.)*

This of course is an ironic comment on the previous grandiloquent outburst. The stranger then leaves the ground and in the hazy sunshine makes for a meadow with a lake in its far end. There he waits, smiling to himself; a barge approaches on the lake and the stranger enters it; it then sails away to the sound of merry song and laughter, the words of the song being—

> *Druan gwŷr! nid oes gradd o naddunt*
> *A ddeil ar beth ond addoli'r bunt!*

(Poor people! every group among them value money above all else.)

Then in 1934, in his last period of intense activity as a poet he found that the subject for the chair ode in the National Eisteddfod of that year was once more on an Arthurian theme—OGOF ARTHUR *(Arthur's Cave)* this time. The subject intrigued him and he set about composing an ode to amuse himself. He showed it to his friend, the Reverend Tegla Davies, who was at that time editor of the monthly EFRYDYDD *(The Student)*; after much persuasion he reluctantly agreed to have it published over a pseudonym in the August number of that year.

In it he makes use of his great skill in the handling of the strict *cynghanedd* meters, and that with the object of satirising much that he found disappointing or tiresome in the life of Wales at that time. On the pretence of being invited to visit a strange cave he parodies the vocabulary and many of the phrases and expressions in his own early poetry and in that of his many imitators. Much of the satire lies in the way he mixes English and Welsh words and phrases, a practice which had become only too prevalent in much spoken Welsh. Then on the pattern of the famous VISIONS of Ellis Wynne (1703) he describes what he pretended he had seen and heard in this "cave", castigating many practices and movements prominent in Wales at that time, not the least of them the pattern in poetry and versification which he himself had set. True to form, he signed the poem, not as in his early days with a romantic pseudonym but by a parody of a possible Welsh form of the name Don Quixote, or as he wrote it *Don Ciceto* which in itself is a mixture of English and Welsh and meaning "the Don with still a kick in him". But perhaps the most ironic touch of all is that there was no trace of Arthur anywhere in the cave!

In following the fascination that the Arthurian theme had for him we have passed by two other major poems that certainly deserve attention. In 1927, soon after ANATIOMAROS, another long poem almost on the same metrical pattern appeared with the title ARGOED. The main difference in form was that four three-line verses with which the poem opens are repeated almost verbatim at the end, thus underlining the poignant situation at the end of the tale.

Argoed takes us, to start with, to a society very similar to the one we met in ANATIOMAROS except that the clan of Arofan live in Argoed, somewhere in the remote forests of Gaul in the first century B.C. Their land has not yet been ravaged and plundered by the Roman invaders; the picture once again is of a pastoral people living an idyllic life, following the needs of the seasons as they come and go, and paying great respect to the accumulated wisdom of their elders and their traditions as an independent people:

THOMAS GWYNN JONES

Hela, bugeilio, fel y bâi galwad,
Dioddef a byw yn ôl deddfau bywyd,
Heb ofni methiant, heb ofyn moethau,
Heb fynnu trais a heb ofni treisiwr;
Magu o do i do yn dawel
Feibion nerth a merched prydferthwch;
Adrodd hanesion dewredd hen oesau,
Bod yn astud a gwybod iawn ystyr
Geiriau y doethion a'r gwŷr da hwythau,
A dirgel feddwl eu mydr gelfyddyd.

(They lived by hunting and herding as the need arose,
Suffering patiently according to the rules of living,
Without fear of failure and expecting no luxuries,
Neither causing violence nor fearing an oppressor;
Raising one generation after another in peace—
Mighty sons and fair young daughters.
They also recounted the brave deeds of old times
Listening carefully and observing the true meaning
Of the words of their wise men and worthy leaders,
And the mysteries of the modes of their literary art).

But little do they realise how soon they will find their most cherished traditions undermined. It was the custom for their poets to visit the main centres of neighbouring clans and there tell their tales and declaim their poems. One day one of their most respected authors goes as usual to an important gathering in the town of Alesia which has at last fallen to the enemy. He had always been honoured and rewarded there, but this time after making his contribution in the language of his people and of the Alesians his audience pretend they do not understand the language he speaks; they snub and humiliate him—not in his and their native language but in a vulgar or pidgin form of Latin. These people had rejected their honourable inheritance, and had embraced a foreign yoke and an alien culture: this the poet can not stand, and so with a laugh of despair he returns to his own people in Argoed:

> *Na'i ddull na'i iaith ni ddeallen' weithion,*
> *Am ei ganiad ni chaffai amgenach*
> *Na thaeog wên wrth ei chwith oganu*
> *â di-raen lediaith o druan Ladin—*
> *Yn ofer aethai ei lafur weithion!*

> *(They no longer understood his manners or his language,*
> *And for his poem he received nothing better*
> *Than a servile grin as they cruelly mocked him*
> *In a corrupt and barbarous form of bastard Latin—*
> *Indeed, all his work and effort had been in vain!)*

But the people of Argoed are not prepared to yield to the invader or to pay him tribute. Rather than do so they set fire to their property and move to another region beyond his reach. This they do with no member of the clan defaulting and with the result:

> *Hyd na welid o'u hôl ond anialwch*
> *Du o ludw lle bu Argoed lydan*

> *(That there was nothing to be seen after them*
> *But a dark expanse of ashes where spacious Argoed had once stood.)*

The symbolism here, I think, is fairly obvious. It is a bitter attack on the Wales of this century, but it has been anchored to an incident which is related of a certain tribe in Gaul in the time when the Romans were occupying it. The dreadful troubles in Ireland in its determined struggle earlier in the century to gain independence were in the recesses of the poet's and other people's minds when he composed this poem. It has therefore overtones of a romantic antiquity as well as of a real present. And whereas in ANATIOMAROS the tone was grave but serene, in ARGOED it is hard and bitterly ironical. The pastoral life depicted in the first part of the poem is romantically ideal; by the end it has been devastated, leaving only a vast expanse of ashes and desert. The poet composed no poem afterwards in which a land of bliss like AFALLON or TÍR NA N-ÓG or any kind of an Arcadian existence figured: he could not, for he himself had set fire to it, and in the light of his experience it would be idle any longer to think of one.

After the publication of ARGOED in 1927 there was a period of nearly seven years before T. Gwynn Jones produced any other major poem. Then in 1934, in the monthly YR EFRYDYDD, which I mentioned above in connection with the OGOF ARTHUR satire, poems started to appear regularly over the pseudonym *Rhufawn*. It soon became apparent from the style and craftsmanship, that the real author was T. Gwynn Jones. They showed an important departure from his previous poetry in that they were no longer written in the strict *cynghanedd* verse forms, but in *vers libre* or free verse. Yet it was free verse with a difference; following his conviction that *cynghanedd* within the line was of the very genius of the language, he kept it in this new verse. Whereas in ordinary free verse line division can often seem anything if not arbitrary, the use of *cynghanedd* not only varied the rhythm of lines but marked out the limits of the pattern of each line, giving it, whether short or long, an entity which in more "regular" verse is conveyed by the number of stresses or syllables or rhyme pattern. Here is a short paragraph from the poem CYNDDILIG to illustrate: I have italicised the letters which show the *cynghanedd* pattern (i.e., consonantal correspondence or some kind of internal rhyme) and have marked the stressed syllables in the line:

> Hei*b*io'*r ll*é y *b*u'*r ll*ýs
> A'i *l*awé*n*ydd diofa*l* únwaith
> Y*ml*ús*g*ai, yn dr*w*m ei *l*és*g*edd,
> he*n* ẃr y*n* ei wáe,
> he*b r*ým, ar ei faglan *b*rén,
> o *g*ám i *g*ám yn ei *g*ẃman,
> ei húnyn únig.

(Past the place where the court used to be, with its once carefree merriment, an old man, weighed down by infirmity and grief ambled by, leaning on his wooden stick, step by step and bent, by himself, alone.)

These poems were later collected in a separate volume and published under the title Y DWYMYN in 1944. It would be impossible for me to think of doing justice to this collection of poems, so I shall confine myself to an analysis of just one of them —CYNDDILIG—one of the master's best poems in the judgement of many of his admirers.

The poem had its origins back in the mid-twenties, in particular from reading and pondering over the implications of the meaning of a three-line verse from the Llywarch Hen cycle of poems which belonged to about the middle of the ninth century. T. Gwynn Jones interpreted the ancient poem thus:

You are in holy orders, you are not a layman,
You will not be called upon to be leader in the day of danger,
Indeed, Cynddilig, you should have been a woman!

And he imagined it was the old warrior, Llywarch Hen, here addressing his son Cynddilig and scorning him for having become a priest or monk, thereby avoiding having to serve in the wars as all Llywarch's other sons had done. They had all been killed in battles against the Saxons, all except Cynddilig and Gwên, the youngest, who was also a warrior. With this idea as a germ, and his own experience and conviction, together with the new pacifist and civil disobedience movements very much in his mind in that period, a symbolic story took root in his imagination.

An outline of the story in the poem goes something like this:
A solitary monk or priest is seen in the moonlight searching for someone among the remains on a battlefield near the ford at Rhyd Forlas somewhere in Powys. Eventually he finds two bodies, each with his dagger in the other. He sees that one of them is his brother Gwên, Gwên the bravest and gentlest of companions. Cynddilig, despite the fact that by conviction he would have nothing to do with war or violence of any kind, is so incensed at his brother's death that he withdraws the dagger from the dead "enemy"

and thrusts it back deep into the man's heart. He then recalls his father's scornful words to him. But full of contrition he also recalls the days when he and Gwên were children together, how Gwên used to play with his tame pigeons; but now he is dead, and without a smile *(gwên)* on his lips. Fear, thinks Cynddilig, being the root cause of man's aggressiveness, had brought these two young men to their death.

Cynddilig then sets about burying the two bodies near the ford, using stones from an old burial cairn nearby to cover them, stones which had before been used to cover other men who had fallen victims of the same kind of fear.

Then we see their father Llywarch Hen himself, bent with age and leaning on a stick, wandering in an area of Powys devastated by war. He recalls that he has lost all his children in these wars, all but one, perhaps, the one that was different from the others. Now there were only the two of them, he himself and that son, neither of them of any use against the enemy.

In his loneliness Llywarch wanders through ruins he well remembers as happy homes, and recalls his son Gwên with his white pigeons; but he cannot find him. Suddenly he hears someone calling "Father" to him, and he thinks it must be Gwên, though he thinks he has heard that Gwên has been killed at Rhyd Forlas. So perhaps it is Cynddilig, the only one left him of all his sons, and he should have been a woman! His son tells him he has been searching for him and that he wants to take him to the shelter of the monastery at Meifod. The old man will not hear of it, wishing to die in battle as his sons had done, all of them but one . . .

The scene changes to the monastery precincts. A young Mercian slave-girl has just rushed over the wall into the monastery grounds and falls at the feet of Llywarch, begging for protection. Cynddilig, the monk, moves between the girl and her pursuers asking them why they hound a helpless and unarmed slave-girl. The pursuers are perplexed by his behaviour; is he brave or just mad? Meanwhile he turns to nurse the girl's wounds while her enemies one by one steal away in shame, all except one; and he draws his bow and hits Cynddilig in the heart before moving away. Cynddilig, without uttering a sound, but crossing himself, falls dead at his father's feet.

The old man is overwhelmed, and in his loss declares he must grieve for Cynddilig, for he never wavered in the face of the enemy but gave his life for a slave-girl:

> ". . . a chan buost fab im ni thechaist;
> Ofered fu roi dy fywyd
> er mwyn fy nghaethes o'r Mers! . . .
> Och, Gynddilig, na buost unben
> a elwid yn nydd rhaid,
> ti, nad eiddot oedd
> nag arf
> nag ofn."

(And as you were a son of mine you wavered not, but what a waste to give your life for a mere slave-girl from Mercia! Indeed, Cynddilig, you should have been called to lead in time of need, you who had neither weapon nor fear.)

Such is the story which grew from a cryptic verse into a tale told with compassion, restraint, and emotion. Some of the other poems in the volume are, in my opinion, less successful. The titles of some of them are FEAR, MYSTERY, HUMANKIND, all of them abstract terms; they do not have a concrete, symbolic or legendary frame as have the other major and more "realised" poems. His genius as a poet was his ability to create and compose, to conjure up a scene or situation rather than an ability to analyse and probe the actions and motives of his fellow men.

It has only been possible to mention a small part of what he wrote, for his long record as a journalist and the sheer volume of his prose and poetry show that he was the most prolific writer of his time in Welsh. A great number of his shorter poems are every bit as significant and as profound in content and skilled in form as the longer ones to which I have referred here. In addition, in later life, he wrote poems of great charm to delight his grandchildren; these show a remarkable ability to enter into the fantasy world of children, and also show the same metrical skill and respect for the idiom of the language as is to be found in the long poems that we have dealt with.

No account of the work of Gwynn Jones would be complete without mention of the enormous amount of work that he translated into Welsh from other languages. He had a remarkable facility in mastering a language, and in his early days translated much from Aeschylus and Homer and Horace into the *cynghanedd* metres in Welsh. Later, in cooperation with a colleague, Professor H. J. Rose, well known to all classicists, he produced a small volume—BLODAU O HEN ARDD *(Flowers from an Old Garden)*—which contains translations into Welsh of some gems of Greek and Latin epitaphs and epigrams, all done into *cynghanedd* verse forms. It would be tedious to enumerate all the works that he translated, but two deserve special mention: first an anthology of native Irish poetry in a small volume entitled AWEN Y GWYDDYL *(The Muse of the Gaels)*; the other, which a competent scholar like the late Sir Idris Bell reckoned a remarkable performance, was a rendering of the first part of Goethe's FAUST for the series CYFRES Y WERIN (a sort of EVERYMAN'S LIBRARY). He was also a great reader and admirer of Dante and wrote the preface to a Welsh rendering of the DIVINE COMEDY by his friend Daniel Rees early in the century. A long list of translations from many languages both in published form and from among his unpublished papers stand to his credit. This would also be an incomplete treatise if no mention were made of his ventures in the world of drama. In the early years of this century, when Welsh drama was in a very rudimentary state, he composed a historical play on a crisis in the life of Dafydd ap Gruffydd, the surviving brother of Llywelyn the Last Prince. It is in prose, but the dialogue is stiff and formal and the longer speeches tend to have the rhythm of free verse rather than that of the spoken language. Later in life he wrote other plays like ANRHYDEDD *(Honour)* but although it deals in a way with the same theme as his poem ANATIOMAROS, it lacks the sweep and conviction of the poetry. In the thirties he collaborated with the musician Mr W. S. Gwynn Williams, to write the libretto for a short musical play—Y GAINC

OLAF *(The Last Song)*—showing how the religious revivals around 1800 were adopting and usurping more and more the old popular folk melodies and using them for the words composed to express the new religious experiences. He also translated two plays by Hugo von Hofmannsthal into Welsh, and these were performed at the National Eisteddfod—POBUN *(Everyman)* in 1933 and LLWYFAN Y BYD *(The World as a Stage)* in 1936.

The reader will have gathered by now that T. Gwynn Jones was a prolific writer and an industrious worker. His published work in book form consists of four volumes of poetry, two substantial biographies, five volumes of essays, studies and reminiscences, and one volume in English on Welsh Folklore. At the beginning of his career in the University he produced a scholarly study of the work of the early bards and the relation between Bardism and the Romances. Later, for years, he was engaged in collecting the poems of Tudur Aled, a late fifteenth century poet; all these poems are scattered in dozens of manuscripts in various libraries with many variant readings, and they needed to be collated before a reliable text could be established. This entailed work on about a hundred-and-fifty poems, totalling in all probability, about eight thousand lines. To this established text of the poems the editor added a hundred page scholarly introduction, together with two hundred pages of notes and commentary. This task took him many years of unremitting toil, but it remains a worthy tribute to his industry and scholarship.

He retired from his academic post in 1937 and had many honours bestowed upon him: the C.B.E. in the Civil List, Doctorates from two Universities, the Cymmrodorion Medal, and from the contributions of a vast number of admirers, a national testimonial presented to him in the National Eisteddfod at Denbigh in 1944. After some years of increasing infirmity he died in 1949 in his seventy-eighth year, and was buried in Aberystwyth. A special memorial issue of the literary periodical *Y Llenor* was published in his honour in the same year.

It has not been possible in a short study such as this to deal adequately with the many aspects of his thought and work. The reader will undoubtedly have noticed that "the lost paradise" or "pleasant land" is a recurring theme in one form or another in his major poems and some of the shorter lyrics like RHOS Y PERERINION *(The Pilgrim's Moorland)*. As Professor T. J. Morgan has shown, this theme and the respect in which he seems to have held medieval Catholicism were used by him "as a kind of scourge to flog the Philistinism and religious self-esteem and prejudices of his own age".

Another tendency which became prominent in his later work is a quest for some sort of serenity of mind and spirit in contrast to the intense passions of youth. Despite the fact that he composed a great number of epigrams which are often caustic and cruel, I do not think that this was his true voice; its product was often nothing but an arid cynicism when he was trying in Yeats's words to find "a little wisdom to take the place of the passion I once had".

It now remains to say a few words in conclusion about his aims and his method. In the foreword which he wrote to a selection of his poems that he made in 1926, he states:

As these poems are only an attempt to give expression to experiences, often very different from one another, without any attempt to reconcile those experiences with any one profession of belief, the experienced reader will see that it would be futile to try to find in them any set doctrine or philosophy.

The only further useful comment then that one can make is to say some words about his style. And it must be stated at the beginning that he found the traditional literary vocabulary of the language fully adequate to the subjects that he dealt with. The Welsh language has a wealth of verbal and other endings and vowel changes, and T. Gwynn Jones exploited to the full the brevity and clarity that are possible because of the syntactical structure of its sentence forms. His sheer virtuosity in expressing himself in the telling of a tale, let us say, within the most complex *cynghanedd* line and verse is often astounding. The prose language and style of the biographies and the novels is direct and crystal clear, but in some of his shorter essays it is sometimes self-consciously formal, or as one reviewer put it: "the style is like a stained glass window, beautiful in itself but not very helpful to see things through it". It can perhaps be said that this great care that he bestowed on the language in its syntax and vocabulary was itself a form of romanticism, but there was a constant tension between the poet's romantic imagination and his strong urge towards a highly formal linguistic and metrical expression. But it was not a static attachment for set forms. As his own record shows, from the strictly conventional metrical forms of YMADAWIAD ARTHUR in 1902 to the cynghanedd controlled free verse of CYNDDILIG in 1934, there has been a great and radical development. He had been constantly looking for new metrical methods of expression but had insisted that they should evolve and develop, in accordance with the genius of the language, from the traditional metres and verse forms.

This romantic imagination worked in the direction of visualising and externalising the ideas that came to him, so it was only natural that the world of external nature should figure extensively in all his poetry. Autumn, for example, was for him the season when the exuberant and prodigal energy and growth of spring and summer were being brought under control in its subdued colours and its abundance of ripe fruit. In the same way the exact and careful use of language and the discipline of *cynghanedd* and the strict metres subdued material which would be mere prose and idle fiction without it.

I have written little of him as a person; that task will have to wait for a full account of his life and work to be produced. Some things stand out however, his remarkable eye for colour and the way he reacted to the scene as a challenge to him to express it in words. He was an exceptional correspondent, replying to letters promptly and at great length without regard to the age or occupation of the person who had first written to him. In his academic work he was first and foremost a "teacher" rather than a "lecturer", delighting his audience with lengthy quotations from a poet he would be discussing, and reciting the poetry not in any form of incantatory style, but stressing the meaning of the words and the sequence of the thought. But it is as a poet of a rare imagination, great versatility, and a superb skill in handling his native tongue that we remember him, and his own description of that rejected poet in his poem ARGOED, fits him best—the poet—

> *Hwnnw a ganodd ei hen ogoniant*
> *A drodd hanesion dewredd hen oesau,*
> *Geiriau y doethion a'r gwŷr da hwythau,*
> *A dirgel foddau eu mydr gelfyddyd,*
> *Yn newydd gân a gynyddai ogoniant*
> *Ei wlad a'i hanes, a chlod ei heniaith.**

**The poet who sang of (his people's) ancient glory and who transformed the stories of the brave men of old and the words of the wise men and good leaders and the mysterious form of their literary craft into a new song that enhanced the glory of their history and the good name of their language.*

A Selected Bibliography

T. GWYNN JONES

A fairly full list of the poet's published work is contained in the 'memorial' number of Y LLENOR, Vol. xxviii, no. 2, Summer 1949, edited by W. J. Gruffydd and T. J. Morgan and published by Hughes and Son, Wrexham. But there is no guide available to the vast number of the signed articles that he wrote for literary magazines and periodicals over a period of more than fifty years.

POETRY

GWLAD Y GÂN A CHANIADAU ERAILL. Caernarfon, Swyddfa'r Herald, 1902.

MANION. Wrecsam, Hughes a'i Fab, 1932.

CANIADAU. Wrecsam, Hughes a'i Fab, 1934.

Y DWYMYN. Gwasg Aberystwyth, 1944.

PROSE

EMRYS AP IWAN, COFIANT. Caernarfon, 1912.

COFIANT THOMAS GEE. Dinbych, Gee a'i Fab, 1913.

Y MÔR CANOLDIR A'R AIFFT. Caernarfon, 1913.

LONA. Wrecsam, Hughes a'i Fab, 1923.

JOHN HOMER. Wrecsam, Hughes a'i Fab, 1923.

CYMERIADAU. Wrecsam, Hughes a'i Fab, 1933.

BEIRNIADAETH A MYFYRDOD. Wrecsam, Hughes a'i Fab, 1935.

ASTUDIAETHAU. Wrecsam, Hughes a'i Fab, 1937.

BRITHGOFION. Llandybie, Llyfrau'r Dryw, 1944.

SCHOLARSHIP

BARDISM AND ROMANCE. London, Cymmrodorion, 1914.

GWAITH TUDUR ALED. Caerdydd, Gwasg Prifysgol Cymru, 1926.

WELSH FOLKLORE AND FOLK-CUSTOM. London, Methuen, 1930.

TRANSLATIONS

MACBETH (Shakespeare) in CYMRU, LI, 1916.

AWEN Y GWYDDYL (From the Irish). Caerdydd, 1923.

GHOSTS (Ibsen). Swansea, Morgan and Higgs, 1920.

FAUST (Goethe). Caerdydd, 1922.

EVERYMAN (Hofmannsthal). Wrecsam, 1933.

GWELEDIGAETHAU'R BARDD CWSG (Ellis Wynne). Translated into English by T. Gwynn Jones, The Gregynog Press, 1940.

BIOGRAPHY

No biography of the poet has yet been published, but there are several tributes to him in the 'memorial' issue of Y LLENOR mentioned above.

CRITICAL

There have been no book-length studies of T. Gwynn Jones. There are valuable articles on some aspects of his work in the already mentioned LLENOR of 1949. Other useful studies of his poetry are to be found in the books listed below:

Thomas Parry: LLENYDDIAETH GYMRAEG, 1900–1945. Lerpwl, Gwasg y Brython 1945.

Sir Idris Bell in the chapter which he added in his English translation of Thomas Parry's HANES LLENYDDIAETH GYMRAEG: THE HISTORY OF WELSH LITERATURE, Oxford, 1955.

Alun Llywelyn Williams: Y NOS, Y NIWL A'R YNYS, Caerdydd, Gwasg Prifysgol Cymru, 1960.

Wenna F. Williams. CERDDI MAWR T. GWYNN JONES in YSGRIFAU BEIRNIADOL, III and IV. Dinbych, Gee. 1967, 1969.

Geraint Bowen: GWŶR LLÊN, Llundain, Griffiths, 1948.

W. Beynon Davies: T. GWYNN JONES, Llandybie, Gwasg y Dryw, 1962.

Anthony Conran has given us a sensitive English translation of the ARGOED poem in THE PENGUIN BOOK OF WELSH VERSE (1967) pp. 230-36.

Acknowledgements

As I was privileged to be a student of his at the University, I am naturally first and foremost indebted for many a view and interpretation to T. Gwynn Jones himself. Later I derived great profit from some lectures on the poet's work given by Mr Saunders Lewis at Aberystwyth in the late forties. Professor T. J. Morgan of the University College, Swansea, read the essay in typescript and suggested many improvements of phrase and of comment, and I am deeply grateful to him for the trouble he took over it. I must also thank Mr Arthur ap Gwynn for most readily allowing me to quote extensively from his father's work. Likewise William Collins and Sons of Glasgow for giving me leave to quote Mr D. Myrddin Lloyd's translation of the three verses to AVALLON from A BOOK OF WALES published by them.

Finally I must record my debt to my wife Mary who not only very patiently typed the whole essay but also scanned and criticised many a woolly phrase and statement, saving me from many pitfalls. But any inelegancies and shortcomings that still remain must be entirely my responsibility.

The Author

W. BEYNON DAVIES is a native of the Vale of Aeron in Cardiganshire. After graduating at the University College of Wales, Aberystwyth, in 1929 he was appointed to the staff of Llandovery College as Welsh Master. In 1944 he joined the staff of Ysgol Ramadeg Ardwyn, Aberystwyth, where he has been head of the Welsh Department since 1960.

*This Edition,
designed by Jeff Clements,
is set in Monotype Spectrum 12 Didot on 13 point
and printed on Basingwerk Parchment by
Qualitex Printing Limited, Cardiff*

It is limited to 750 copies of which this is

Copy No.
545.

4548